Medicine for Winners

DR. D. K. OLUKOYA

Warfare Prayer Series 27

MEDICINE

FOR

WINNERS

MEDICINE FOR WINNERS
© 2005 DR. D. K. OLUKOYA
ISBN: 978-38233-6-1
1st Printing – July 2005 AD

_ hed by:
The Battle Cry Christian Ministries
11, Gbeto Street, Off Iyana Church Bus Stop, Iwaya Road, Iwaya, Yaba, P.O. Box 12272, Ikeja, Lagos.
Website: www.battlecrying.com
Email: battlecrying@representattive.com
Phone: 0803-304-4239, 0803-332-2376, 0803-306-0073, 0802-303-3938, 0803-309-8246, 0803-315-7249, 0803-305-4142.

FOREIGN CORRESPONDENCES
UNITED STATES
Phone: 404 – 454 – 3358

GHANA
Phone: 24236113

All scripture quotation is from the King James version of the Bible.

Cover Illustration: Sis Shade Olukoya
All rights reserved.
We prohibit reproduction in whole or part without written permission.

TABLE OF CONTENTS

1. MEDICINE FOR WINNERS..................................4

2. WHAT THE WINNERS KNOW...................... 17

3. CHARACTERISTICS OF LOSERS.................... 30

4. THIS DECREE SHALL NOT FAIL................... 41

5. THE UNCHALLENGEABLE VICTORY............. 53

6. PRAYER POINTS FOR WINNERS 63

Chapter One

MEDICINE FOR WINNERS

If I ask you who needs medicine, you are likely to say it is the sick. Medicine is generally associated with sickness. Most people don't know that the healthy also need medicine to remain healthy. You don't have to suffer shortage of blood before you take blood capsules or blood tonic. There are blood medicines that do other works in the body, rather than giving you more blood. The side of the Lord Jesus is a winning side. You are a winner on the side of Jesus. Since the desire of your heart is to remain a winner, you are going to discover the medicine for winners in this book.

Ps. 8:1-9: O LORD our Lord, how excellent is thy name in all the earth! who hast set thy glory above the heavens. Out of the mouth of babes and sucklings hast thou ordained strength because of thine enemies, that thou mightest still the enemy and the avenger. When I consider thy heavens, the work of thy fingers, the moon and the stars, which thou hast ordained; What is man, that thou art mindful of him? and the son of man, that thou visitest him? For thou hast made him a little lower than the angels, and hast crowned him with glory and honour. Thou madest him to have dominion over the works of thy hands; thou hast put all things under his feet: All sheep and oxen, yea, and the beasts of the field; The fowl of the air, and the fish of the sea, and whatsoever passeth through the paths of the seas. O LORD our Lord, how excellent is thy name in all the earth!.

We are serving an excellent God. The name of the Lord is excellent in all the earth. There is no god whose name is that excellent. Some gods are only popular among a few worshippers in some corners of the world. The creator of the heavens and the earth is excellent in glory, excellent in power and excellent in honour. God wants you to excel as He is excellent. Man occupies a special position in the works of God. Verse six of the above text says God made man to have dominion over the works of His hands.

Go back to verse three of the text. The heavens, the moon and the stars are part of God's works that He has ordained man to have dominion over. In verses seven and eight, all sheep and oxen and beasts of the field, and fowls of the air, and fish of the sea, and all that passes through the paths of the seas are brought under the dominion of man. The place of man is unique in creation. He lives in power and dominion over the works of God's hands and glorifies the excellency of the most High. The will of God is for you to share in the excellency of His dominion.

Duet. 28:13: And the LORD shall make thee the head, and not the tail and thou shalt be above only, and thou shalt not be beneath; if that thou hearken unto the commandments of the LORD thy

God, which I command thee this day, to observe and to do them.

Exercising dominion is to be above only. Where we read before in Psalms eight verse six, we learnt that God "has put all things under" the feet of man. This is simply a different way of expressing the dominion that God intends for man. The head is above all other members of the body. God wants you to be the head and to remain above all. You can reach the top and remain there. This is the excellency of the power and wisdom of God in all the earth. The Most High wants you to be a winner. Winners are people described below.

Rom. 8:37: Nay, in all these things we are more than conquerors through him that loved us.

A winner is someone that's more than a conqueror. A conqueror must fight to win a battle. He goes on to divide the spoils and to hold captive the prisoners of war. But someone more than a conqueror does not have to go through all that. If a conqueror fights to win, a person more than a conqueror will only speak to win a battle. If a conqueror has to hold prisoners of war captive, a more than conqueror will only stand and his enemies will rush to and submit to him. In the book of

Colossians chapter two, there is another description of who a winner is.

Col. 2:15: And you, being dead in your sins and the uncircumcision of your flesh, hath he quickened together with him, having forgiven you all trespasses.

You are a winner if you are practically walking in the victory of Jesus Christ explained above. Winning is not all about coming first in a race or taking the lead in a competition. You can be a winner in an examination and be subject to the harassment of witches and wizards. You can be a winner in a race and be put on the run by powers of darkness. A spiritual winner is a winner indeed. The victory of Jesus on the cross guarantees your winning in every area and contest of life. That victory makes you a true winner in the Lord Jesus Christ.

A winner is someone noted for outstanding and unusual accomplishments. A winner is someone who never gives up at all but keeps fighting. A writer puts it this way "A winner never quits and a quitter never wins." Giving up will make you a loser. A winner is someone who pursues, overtakes and recovers from the enemies. Pause a little and take these winners'

PRAYER POINTS.

- I pursue my oppressors, I overtake them, and I recover my property from them in the name of Jesus.

- I pursue the strong man, I overtake him and recover my gifts from his hands in the name of Jesus.

A winner is someone above adversities. Adversities come, but he triumphs over them. Many people have been swept off their feet by winds of adversities. On the troubled sea, Jesus demonstrated the power of a winner. He woke up from sleep and rebuked the sea. The Bible says, "there was a great calm". A winner will see storms, adversities, troubles and tribulations, but he will triumph over them all.

Matt 8:26: And he saith unto them, Why are ye fearful, O ye of little faith? Then he arose, and rebuked the winds and the sea; and there was a great calm.

A winner is someone whose strength is great enough to withstand the power of opposition. A winner is somebody who does not fail in the days of adversity. Adversities sink the faith of some people. Many people faint in the days of adversity. The Bible says those who faint in the day of adversities have small strength.

Winners have gone beyond that level.

Prov 24:10: If thou faint in the day of adversity, thy strength is small.

A winner is somebody who is above poverty, worry depression, frustration, fear and sin. God is still in the business of substitution. He can remove anybody in the interest of His children. God will not hesitate to remove your oppressors, no matter who they are, and replace them with people that will favour you. God will not mind to remove your tormentors and replace them with people that will cherish you. He can remove those standing against your progress and replace them with people that will facilitate it. God fights on behalf of winners to keep them at the top.

At a time when there was famine in Israel, Elijah was a winner whom God supernaturally sustained. At a brook, he was fed by ravens, but when the brook dried up, he was supernaturally linked up with a widow woman. The situation still looked deadly, but the last meal of the widow was multiplied. This is the experience of winners in the face of famine and poverty. God will always make a way out. The economy and finances of winners are regulated by the Heaven of heaven. They live above the dictates of power policies.

1King 17:5-9: So he went and did according unto the word of the LORD: for he went and dwelt by the brook Cherith, that is before Jordan. And the ravens brought him bread and flesh in the morning, and bread and flesh in the evening; and he drank of the brook. And it came to pass after a while, that the brook dried up, because there had been no rain in the land. And the word of the LORD came unto him, saying, Arise, get thee to Zarephath, which belongeth to Zidon, and dwell there: behold, I have commanded a widow woman there to sustain thee.

A renowned New Testament prophet stood and declared the counsel of the Holy Ghost to Paul. What prophet Agabus revealed was frightening. He saw bondage, imprisonment, beatings, assault, false accusation, fiery persecution, injustice and all manners of ill treatment against Paul in Jerusalem. Any other person could be gripped with fear on hearing such revelation from a tested and respected prophet like Agabus. In fact, the people around Paul advised him to think twice about the journey. But Paul was a winner who lived above fear. The more they tried to dissuade him, the more he was determined to go. A winner can never be pushed back by the fear of the known and the unknown. No matter what, he will continue to forge ahead.

Acts 21:10-14: And as we tarried there many days, there came down from Judaea a certain prophet, named Agabus. And when he was come unto us, he took Paul's girdle, and bound his own hands and feet, and said, Thus saith the Holy Ghost, So shall the Jews at Jerusalem bind the man that owneth this girdle, and shall deliver him into the hands of the Gentiles. And when we heard these things, both we, and they of that place, besought him not to go up to Jerusalem. Then Paul answered, What mean ye to weep and to break mine heart? for I am ready not to be bound only, but also to die at Jerusalem for the name of the Lord Jesus. And when he would not be persuaded, we ceased, saying, The will of the Lord be done.

A time came in the life and ministry of Samuel that he stood to challenge all Israel asking them to point to sin in his life if they could find any. He was a winner that lived above sin. He did not care what anybody might say because he was sure he had no skeleton in his cupboard. There was silence everywhere after Samuel spoke. Nobody in the whole country could point to unrighteousness in his life. He stands as an example of a winner of all time.

1Sam. 12:3-4: Behold, here I am: witness against me before the LORD, and before his anointed: whose ox have I taken? or whose ass have I taken? or whom have I defrauded? whom have I oppressed? or of whose hand have I received any bribe to blind mine eyes therewith? and I will restore it you. And they said, Thou hast not defrauded us, nor oppressed us, neither hast thou taken ought of any man's hand.

A winner is somebody the Bible describes as an overcomer. When others are talking about defeat, he is talking about abundance of victory. The faith you have in Jesus Christ as the son of God makes you an overcomer.

1John. 5:4-5: For whatsoever is born of God overcometh the world: and this is the victory that overcometh the world, even our faith. Who is he that overcometh the world, but he that believeth that Jesus is the Son of God?.

The choice is yours to become a winner. The Bible says that whatsoever is born of God is a winner. Whosoever is born of God is a winner. You can choose to be among the whosoever. It does not discriminate against anybody. Irrespective of your religion, race, class, status, etc., a winner is somebody who has faith

in the Lord Jesus Christ. He is truly an overcomer. But the opposite of a winner is a loser. Faith in yourself as if you don't need God, faith in friends, background, people, etc will continue to make you a loser.

Rev. 21:7: He that overcometh shall inherit all things; and I will be his God, and he shall be my son.

A winner is an inheritor of all things as shown in the above verse. All things include "ALL THINGS!" Nothing is impossible for an overcomer to inherit. He will overcome all things in this world and in the world to come. A winner will inherit God and will inherit an eternal sonship with God. God is the origin and creator of all things. If you have God, you have everything. A winner has everything because he has God.

A winner is somebody who has completely handed over the management of his life to Jesus Christ. He is no more the Lord of his own life as he realizes he had lost the ownership of his life to Jesus and surrenders himself perpetually to His Lordship. He does not just call Jesus, "Lord!" to honour Him by mere words but demonstrates his submission to Him by doing everything He commands.

Luke 6:46: And why call ye me, Lord, Lord, and do not the things which I say?

A winner is somebody that is rid of unbelief. He does not doubt God because he has come to a point at which his trust in the Lord is unshakeable. Everybody in the world may have a contrary opinion of something but his His own position is determined by what God says about the situation. A winner does not ask God if He means what He says or not. He knows that God is not a man to waste words or to lie.

Luke 6:46: And why call ye me, Lord, Lord, and do not the things which I say?

A winner is somebody who wins the battles of life. Different battles confront different people in the world. But the world is only interested in celebrating those that overcome their battles. One hundred competitors may participate in a race, but only the winners are celebrated. Jesus is celebrated in heaven and on earth because He has overcome the battles of life.

Rev. 3:21: To him that overcometh will I grant to sit with me in my throne, even as I also overcame, and am set down with my Father in his throne.

Chapter Two

WHAT THE WINNERS KNOW

Nobody becomes a winner without a good knowledge of how to win in a specific area of life. Winners are knowledgeable hence winners in boxing matches have good knowledge of boxing and how to win. Winners in swimming contests know how to swim and beat their competitors. Winners in long distance race know how to run and reserve energy to carry them on successfully. Winners in spiritual things know certain things that you must learn if you want to join them. If you don't know how to be or remain a winner, your ignorance will cost you very dearly.

Hos 6:4: O Ephraim, what shall I do unto thee? O Judah, what shall I do unto thee? for your goodness is as a morning cloud, and as the early dew it goeth away.

Winners know the following truths which ring in their spirits like a bell.

1. **Satan is a thief and a Liar** - Winners know very well that satan has a mission to steal. They keep everything they have from within his reach. If you are alerted that armed robbers are operating on the road you are traveling, on you are likely to suspend the journey, stop a while, or go ahead in the

company that don't know. They just go on and then fall into diverse dangers.

John 10:10: The thief cometh not, but for to steal, and to kill, and to destroy: I am come that they might have life, and that they might have it more abundantly.

Winners also know that they can't rely on anything that comes from the devil. He is a liar which they ignore. Information is very powerful and so what the devil does is to send wrong or frightening information to people. But winners know that no truth proceeds from the devil. Whatever he says does not matter to them. That is the reason they go on to prosper where others accept the lies of the devil to keep them in poverty. Because they know satan is a lair, they do exploits where others accept satan's verdict that it is not possible to achieve anything.

2. **They are not subject to satan** - Winners know very clearly that the devil has no legal right to control their lives. Having then submitted to the lordship of Jesus Christ, they know that one servant can't be ruled by two masters. Winners know whom they have given their lives to. They know satan is an intruder.

Luke 16:13: No servant can serve two masters: for either he will hate the one, and love the other; or else he will hold to the one, and despise the other. Ye cannot serve God and mammon.

Let me illustrate this point. Every woman knows that the only man that has a legal right over her life and body is her husband. No matter how many males are in her husband's family, she knows that only her husband can touch her in the sense in which a husband intimately relates with his wife. Winners know that they are like wives given over to Jesus and they know satan is a strange man that has no legal right over their lives. You must know who your Lord is if you want to be a winner. Even animals knows their masters.

Isa. 1:3: The ox knoweth his owner, and the ass his master's crib: but Israel doth not know, my people doth not consider.

3. **Possibility of Recovery** - Winners know that it is possible to forcefully recover anything the devil has stolen. They know that the principle of restitution is applicable to getting back their stolen goods from satan. The Bible says a thief should restore whatever he has stolen.

Exodus 22:2-4: If a thief be found breaking up, and be smitten that he die, there shall no blood be shed for him. If the sun be risen upon him, there shall be blood shed for him; for he should make full restitution; if he have nothing, then he shall be sold for his theft. If the theft be certainly found in his hand alive, whether it be ox, or ass, or sheep; he shall restore double.

Winners know that whatever satan steals does not belong to him. If something is yours, you cannot steal it. Nobody challenges you for trying to turn the ignition of your car. Nobody raises an alarm on you for attempting to open your door. Nobody is after you for trying to get a job with your own credentials. It is only a thief that takes what does not belong to him. The verdict of God is that such a thief should restore what he has stolen.

You can force satan to make restitution to you. Everything he has taken from you can be forcefully taken back. Policemen are always armed when they are going after robbers. The robbers themselves are armed to successfully rob the innocent. Satan is armed with lies, threat, sickness, calamities, etc. to rob you of the good things of your life. As no robber goes after useless things, so also satan does not target what is of no value in any life. Winners know they can pursue satan, overtake him and recover everything he has stoles from them.

4. Possibility of Overthrow - Winners are people who know that the seat of satan can be forcefully overthrown and destroyed. Armed robbers are dangerous. They have their hideouts. The police also know they can sack them and overthrow their control in those hideouts. Many times, the police are seen on daring operations, declaring war on robbers and miscreants in their hideouts. The devil is a chief robber. Winners know they can take the battles to the seat of satan in specific areas of their lives and sack him. Jesus also confirms that this is possible in practice.

Luke 11:21: When a strong man armed keepeth his palace, his goods are in peace:

Most people would rather avoid areas they know that satan has established his seat. Some christians would refuse to pray over a sickness they know is an attack from witches and wizards. Not only that the moment some ministers are told that certain powers of darkness are behind a problem, they advise the victim to take heart and accept fate. Winners don't do that. They go straight for satan's seat to overthrow it. If policemen don't sack robbers in their hideouts, they will continue to operate from there and will continue to rob and share their loot. Take this prayer point aggressively as you read on.

- All satanic seats, be destroyed in the name of Jesus.

5. Satan's Targets - All winners know that they are targets of the devil against which he is working seriously. Satan wants to turn current winners to spiritual pampers. They know they cannot afford to give him room to do that. Peter was a winner in the camp of Jesus. He was consequently the target of satan but Jesus warned him that the devil had abandoned all other assignments to concentrate on him alone. He wanted to sift Peter like wheat and leave him useless.

Luke 22:31: And the Lord said, Simon, Simon, behold, Satan hath desired to have you, that he may sift you as wheat.

Winners know they are a big problem to satan. They know that they are known in hell. Winners know they are declared most wanted by the powers of darkness. What satan tried then to do to Peter still tops on his agenda against winners of today. He wants to sift them of their grace, victory, authority, etc and leave them dead and though empty. Winners know the antics of satan and so they are very careful with their lives.

Some Nigerians led the campaign against military rule. They became special targets for the military government. These men became extremely careful in their going out and coming in. There were places they wouldn't go to avoid falling into the hands of their enemies. Winners know they have to avoid certain things in life if they must keep their testimonies.

6. Divine Purpose - Winners are people that know that nothing happens to them by accident. They know that everything in their lives is carefully arranged to fulfil a divine purpose. They are not bothered about whatever comes their ways because they can see the hands of God in all their experiences. They know they have to pass through some trainings in the hands of God.

Rom 8:28: And we know that all things work together for good to them that love God, to them who are the called according to his purpose.

7. **Fear As A great Enemy** – All winners know that fear is a great enemy. Their hearts are made up about whatever God says. They know that fear can make somebody to fall from his realm of exploits. Peter stumbled on the surface of a boisterous sea when he was walking towards Jesus. On the water, Peter already belonged to another class of his own. No other apostle stepped out with him. The moment he was on the waters, he was celebrating a victory in an area where fellow apostles were not qualified to attempt a contest. In the history of mankind, Peter stood above all men ever born of woman, at the moment of walking on the waters. But fear set in and he began to sink.

Matt 14:28-30: And Peter answered him and said, Lord, if it be thou, bid me come unto thee on the water. And he said, Come. And when Peter was come down out of the ship, he walked on the water, to go to Jesus. But when he saw the wind boisterous, he was afraid; and beginning to sink, he cried, saying, Lord, save me.

Fear can bring anybody down from the greatest height. Winners know they don't have any business with fear. The only fear they have is the holy fear of God. They know that fear can put an end to steps of rare exploits. They choose not to look at the anger of the sea waves in the areas of their notable deeds, unlike Peter who feared the waters and was sinking. The servant of Elisha feared the army of the enemies and lost the hope of survivals. Fear kills, paralyses and disgraces. Though fear celebrates satan, winners have overcome all fears.

8. Honesty – Winners know that only losers cover up their sins and pretend as if nothing is wrong when of course, everything is wrong. They are very plain and sincere. They don't hesitate to acknowledge their ignorance, sin, error, failure, etc. This quality marked out David as a specially beloved servant of God. Nathan confronted David over his sin and the king swallowed his pride. He acknowledged his error and confessed it openly.

2 Sam 12:13: And David said unto Nathan, I have sinned against the LORD. And Nathan said unto David, The LORD also hath put away thy sin; thou shalt not die.

Some people think they are too highly placed in the society to acknowledge their sins. Some think they are too respected, and so cannot repent. Some think their position are too classified to make for an open confession of their errors. All of these people remain losers. A winning life is an honest and sincere. A person with such a life does not try to cover up his error wherever it is found. He amends his ways and continues an honest life before God and men. These are winners indeed.

The Christian of today is full of hypocrisies. Sin is so rampant among the children of God, yet every eye shows pretence, every look shows innocence, and every appearance shows honesty. But God knows all secrets, Satan knows and you know it too that your life is not right with God. You will remain a loser except you repent. In counting your losses, you would have lost your respect, honour, dignity, trust, etc. and the worst will be to lose your life in the lake of fire. Winners always keep a short account with God. They examine and review their lives within short intervals.

9. **Every Problem Has a Solution** - Winners know that there is a divine way out of every problem. They don't care about the name, nature and extent of a problem. But despite these, they know there is a way out of every problem. Job didn't know how it

all began. Like a flash of lightening, his life was overturned. He scratched everywhere for answer, but all was in vain. His solution and victory shows that he was a winner indeed.

Job 19:25: For I know that my redeemer liveth, and that he shall stand at the latter day upon the earth:

Like Job, winners know that they have a Redeemer in heaven whose eyes are over them. They know that even though the wasters rage and the storms hit very hard, the Deliverer does not sleep. They know that, though the enemies multiply, God is up to the task. They are not daunted by the size of their problems or the number of their enemies but repose and put their confidence in the God whose ways are past finding out.

10. **God's Speciality** - Winners know that God's speciality is to do the impossible. Towards the end of a university education, students know they have to narrow down their areas of specialization. There are problems in life that only specialists in certain fields can solve. God is a specialist. His area of specialization is the impossible.

Matt 19:26: But Jesus beheld them, and said unto them, With men this is impossible; but with God all things are possible.

Winners don't mind how impossible a situation is because they know that the more impossible a situation is, the better it is for God. The more complex a problem is, the easier for the God's power and wisdom to handle it. Let me surprise you that God deliberately create rooms for impossibilities just to prove His power. A man was born blind. Jesus said it was not because of sin or biological accident. He said God sent him (the blind man) incomplete into the world so that He (God) might complete His work of creation before men. Winners know that impossibilities are God's areas of interest and they know that God never comes in late.

John 9:1-3: And as Jesus passed by, he saw a man which was blind from his birth. And his disciples asked him, saying, Master, who did sin, this man, or his parents, that he was born blind? Jesus answered, Neither hath this man sinned, nor his parents: but that the works of God should be made manifest in him.

Chapter Three

CHARACTERISTICS OF LOSERS

Losers have characteristics. Everything in the world has a mean of identification. You will know losers by the following qualities.

1. Aimless Fight - Losers fight aimlessly. They lack purpose, direction and focus. Ask them why they are fighting and they tell you because others are fighting too. Ask them who they are fighting and they tell you they only know that their aimless punches would hit some persons. Losers keep looking for God from one place to another because they think God is geographically located. They don't understand it when Jesus said that God is a spirit that is available everywhere.

John 4:21-24: Jesus saith unto her, Woman, believe me, the hour cometh, when ye shall neither in this mountain, nor yet at Jerusalem, worship the Father. Ye worship ye know not what: we know what we worship: for salvation is of the Jews. But the hour cometh, and now is, when the true worshippers shall worship the Father in spirit and in truth: for the Father seeketh such to worship him. God is a Spirit: and they that worship him must worship him in spirit and in truth.

2. Backward Movement - Losers move backwardly from one level to another. The book of Jude perfectly

describes their backward movement. Losers are called "wandering stars" that move from one territory of darkness to another.

Jude vs 12-13: These are spots in your feasts of charity, when they feast with you, feeding themselves without fear: clouds they are without water, carried about of winds; trees whose fruit withereth, without fruit, twice dead, plucked up by the roots; Raging waves of the sea, foaming out their own shame; wandering stars, to whom is reserved the blackness of darkness for ever.

3. **Lack of Secrecy** – Losers Can not keep their secrets secret. They reveal their secrets to their enemies and make senseless advertisement of their lives. They are ensnared by the words of their own mouths. In the lives of losers, enemies have a field day because of the information they have about them. Losers don't where to talk and where to keep quiet. If your mouth leaks like a basket, you are in trouble. It is a characteristic of losers to talk into the hands of your enemies.

Matt 12:27: And if I by Beelzebub cast out devils, by whom do your children cast them out? therefore they shall be your judges.

I was very much younger, I sat down to meditate on how senseless it is to do self advertisement. The Juju musicians of those days were found of singing the praise of some individuals considered to be great achieves. I started considering some of the names one after the other. Because these popular music were played on radio, and on the streets, consciously or unconsciously, one becomes aware of that they were saying. I then discovered, with only few exemptions, that many of the names sung about were nowhere to be found. There is no sense in any senseless advertisement.

4. Hypocrisy – All losers cover up their sins. The word of God tells us the implication of covering up one's sins.

Prov 28:13: He that covereth his sins shall not prosper: but whoso confesseth and forsaketh them shall have mercy.

What losers call their privacies are so dirty that they could not be mentioned in the public. Their popular slogan is that if you fail to clean your mouth after meal, people would know what you have eaten. They use such deceptive proverbs to encourage their dishonesty, hypocrisy and insincerity.

5. Burdens – Losers carry their burdens on their

heads. They don't know there is a God in heaven whose responsibility it is to carry burdens. One thing with God is that He carries burdens that are cast upon Him. Losers choose to carry their burdens to the point where everybody that sees them pities them.

Ps 55:22: Cast thy burden upon the LORD, and he shall sustain thee: he shall never suffer the righteous to be moved.

There are burdens you are not supposed to carry at all. I watched a woman pack a few things in a big bag. She also had a very small bag aside the big one. Her daughter of about three years chose to carry the bigger load as they were set to go. She was struggling with it, but couldn't move it at all. Her mother rebuked her and pointed her to the small, light, hand bag meant for her. With ease, she picked it up and they moved. You feel a heaviness on your spirit because you are carrying a burden that is not yours. Losers don't let God do His job; They try to help Him.

6. Unforgiveness – Losers keep account of past offences. They grumble, they murmur and they complain. They have a diary where offences are

recorded. If the same offender crosses their ways, they multiply his or her offences by the number of times they occur. They are not aware that they are working against their own souls.

Mark 11:25-26: And when ye stand praying, forgive, if ye have ought against any: that your Father also which is in heaven may forgive you your trespasses. But if ye do not forgive, neither will your Father which is in heaven forgive your trespasses.

If you keep records of offences, you will lose your peace of mind, your fellowship with God, your concentration, good health, etc. Until you let go of all offences against you, you won't know how much peace you have forfeited.

7. **Quitters** – Losers are quitters. They quit very easily. If they don't have what they are expecting on time, they quit and throw away their patience. In the face of little problems, they give up and prefer to die. Patience is necessary to win the battles of life, but losers never like to be patient.

Heb 10:36: For ye have need of patience, that, after ye have done the will of God, ye might receive the promise.

8. **Unbelieving** – The motto of losers is "seeing is believing." Even when they see victory all around, they go for defeat. They don't believe anything; They don't believe anybody; They don't believe God for His words, and they don't believe that anything good, wonderful miraculous, etc will ever happen.

Rev 21:8: But the fearful, and unbelieving, and the abominable, and murderers, and whoremongers, and sorcerers, and idolaters, and all liars, shall have their part in the lake which burneth with fire and brimstone: which is the second death.

9. **Sidetalks** – Losers are people that are moved by sidetalks. They imagine that every conversation is about them. They fret when they see two people stand to talk.

10. **Satanic Alternatives** – Losers are people that follow satanic roadmaps. They accept satanic alternatives to their problems. What is important to them is for their problems to be solved no matter how or from whom the solution comes.

Losers celebrate self-pity; They walk in the broad way. They hate discipline, self-control or anything that affects their convenience in life. They want to follow God in their own way and want Him to accommodate them and their abominations.

REASONS FOR FAILURE

There are several reasons why brilliant people fail. There are reasons why skillful people don't succeed and there are also reasons why many are sick in the spirit.

1. Purposeless Life – Living a life that floats like a dead fish wastes potentials away. This is a lack of definite, and major purpose. Because they try everything in life, people in this category don't have a definite focus of what they want or what they are living for. A dead fish floats, but a live one can swim against the current. A life controlled by circumstances or environment is a terrible life that wastes potentials and opportunities.

Take this prayer point:
- I refuse to float in the ocean of life in the name of Jesus.

2. Inherited problems – Those who have unfavourable inheritance are endangered by

wastage. If your father had only twelve wives and you are the first child of the tenth woman, you have inherited something that will affect you.

3. Spiritual Indiscipline – Spiritual indiscipline has made many to neglect or waste every opportunity God gave them for their spiritual advancement.

4. Lack of Determination – People with great potentials fail because they lack the determination to rise above their present level. They just decide or accept to remain where they are.

5. Problematic Sickness – Some people just find themselves in problems that border on their health which they cannot explain. Their potentials and prospects waste away in the process.

6. Environmental Influences – Especially at a young age, environmental influences can make a potential winner to become a loser.

7. Inability to Persist – Lack of persistence is responsible for many failures. Success in life does not come easily hence the Bible emphasizes perseverance and persistence as conditions for

success in life.

8. Evil companionship – If your friends are the children of the devil, don't expect God's blessings.

9. Doing the wrong Job – Doing a job you are not supposed to do will make you fail in life. There is a place suitable for you according to God's design of your personality and gifts. So Locate yourself properly as God cannot bless what He did not ask your to do.

10. Wealth of Sorrow – Earning money that is not meant for you can doom your chances in life. Many people possess the wealth of sorrow by exploiting the innocent. They will live only to discover that they have accumulated the wealth to their hurt.

12. Lack of Vision – If you lack a clear direction of where you going in life, you cannot succeed.

13. Gossiping Others – Every evil you speak against others brings you down by degrees.

15. Talkativeness – Excessive talking is the bane of the sorrowful lives which many are living today.

16. Procrastination – Those who postpone what they ought to do to another day never do anything at last.
17. Greed – Greed is a vice that drives people to take what belongs to others. When vengeance is taken, they lose their success.

18. Lack of knowledge of God's word – If you don't know the scriptures very well, you cannot know the mind of God about things concerning you. To succeed then becomes difficult. The Bible says, "Examine yourself". And so the time has come for serious self-examination. Look at your life against everything you have read so far. Discover yourself and begin to pray.

Prayer Points

1. I refuse to inherit any spirit of failure in the name of Jesus.
2. I climb the mountain of promotion in the name of Jesus.
3. Every anti-winner device be paralysed in the name of Jesus.
4. I prophesy fulfilment to all my desires in the name of Jesus.

Chapter Four

THIS DECREE SHALL NOT FAIL

There is power in a decree. A decree is an official command or decision. When a constituted authority passes a decree, the subjects obey. The decree is a major Characteristic of the military government. The military rules by decrees. The official decision or command of the ruling council of a military government passes on as a decree for the whole country to obey.

The word of God says a child of God could function like a unit military government, ruling by decrees. Every believer is a spiritual soldier. In the body of Christ, each Christian has the mandate to pass a decree on any issue. As the ruling council of the military agrees on behalf of the entire military body to pass a decree, honoured and respected by every citizen, so a child of God can pass decrees on behalf of heaven.

Job 22:28: Thou shalt also decree a thing, and it shall be established unto thee: and the light shall shine upon thy ways.

A decree is read to public hearing by only one military officer or ruler. The decree is however the agreement of the whole body of the military. As soon as the decree is passed, the lowest ranking military personnel in the remotest part of the country ensures that it is obeyed. All law enforcement agencies begin to work to enforce the decree. Similarly, when a child of God passes a decree, the whole army of heaven begin to operate to enforce it.

Every decree is backed up by the power of an authority. This is why just anybody cannot issue a decree. If I wake up to announce that all civil servants should not go to work, people would be interested to know my right to do so. Above all, they would want to know if what I said is backed up by the authority of the land. The moment they find out that I am an outlet or representative of the government, which has the power to effectively issue official commands, they would comply at once.

The government of heaven is over and above all. A child of God is a representative of the heavenly government. When a believer therefore issues a decree, all demons in the whole universe know that the decree is backed up by the power of heaven. Satan knows that a decree issued by a child of God is supported by the headquarters of heaven. Both the devil and his demons don't argue, they just comply. People don't have any power against a decree. The worst they can do is to protest. Demons, know that they don't have any power against your decree as a child of God. They may however protest, but don't mind them.

A decree is a stamp of authority. A military ruler who issues a decree does not go everywhere trying to make people obey and submit to the power of the decree. He only announces the decree. He makes sure the citizens are aware of the latest government decision and that settles the matter. A Christian does not have to be running after demons to make sure they obey and submit to him. Only issue a decree and the law enforcement agents of the heavenly headquarters will carry it out.

Another Characteristic of a decree is that no single citizen has the power to change or review it. It takes the existing military government or a succeeding one to change any decree. Even if the decree is made by the smallest number of the constituted authority, it becomes a law. When a child of God issues a decree, no demon can change or review it. Whatever you do with your decrees as a Christian is what heaven stands upon. This is a tremendous power, vested on every child of God. The New Testament does not change the principle. It only presents it in a different language. Jesus said:

Matt 16:19: And I will give unto thee the keys of the kingdom of heaven: and whatsoever thou shalt bind on earth shall be bound in heaven: and whatsoever thou shalt loose on earth shall be loosed in heaven.

If whatever you bind on earth is bound in heaven, it means whatever you decree on earth is established for you in heaven. The decree of a child of God affects the decision and action of heaven. You may be young in age or very old, your decree is treated with the same urgency in heaven. The Lord has proved His faithfulness over the years. Those who know that their decrees are established in heaven do not hesitate to issue one, where the need arises. Elijah is a good example.

1 Kings 17:1: And Elijah the Tishbite, who was of the inhabitants of Gilead, said unto Ahab, As the LORD God of Israel liveth, before whom I stand, there shall not be dew nor rain these years, but according to my word.

Elijah told Ahab that rain would only fall upon the whole country if he decreed it so. He specifically said rain would not fall, if he did not ask or decree it to fall. As soon as Elijah said this, the headquarters of heaven locked up the waters of heaven immediately. False prophets tried to conjure demonic powers to review or change the decree of Elijah but it didn't work. For any demon to change the decree of a believer, it has to prevail against the heavenly headquarters. Of course, this is not possible. The only time rain fell again was when Elijah decreed the waters of heaven to gather and shower upon the land.

1 Kings 18:41: And Elijah said unto Ahab, Get thee up, eat and drink; for there is a sound of abundance of rain.

Kings rule by decrees. Their orders go unchallenged. Anytime anybody dares to challenge the decree of a king, the person stands the risk of losing his life. We have been made kings and priests to God by reason of our faith in the Lord Jesus Christ. Any power standing against your command stands the risk of the wrath of heaven.

Rev 1:6: And hath made us kings and priests unto God and his Father; to him be glory and dominion for ever and ever. Amen.

Heaven is waiting for your decree. If you don't issue any decree, there will be nothing to establish in heaven.

If you don't bind a thing on earth, there will be nothing to bind in heaven. How frequently heaven works and interferes in the affairs of men depends on how often you issue decrees as a child of God. By our decrees, we can do and undo and no court of law in the second heaven, on earth, underneath the earth or in the seas can challenge our decrees.

Many children of God do not recognize the power they have with heaven they do not know the extent of their influence on earth. Those who do, lack the faith to live and operate in the reality of their power to live and operate in the reality of their power. You are operating the power of attorney as a Christian. Use the power as much as possible. It is the responsibility of heaven to carry out your words.

There are many decrees to issue as you read this book. The first decree is found in the book of Isaiah chapter six. It explains the relationship between the life of a king and the visions of a prophet.

Isa. 6:1: *In the year that king Uzziah died I saw also the Lord sitting upon a throne, high and lifted up, and his train filled the temple.*

Uzziah was one of the youngest kings in the Bible. At sixteen, he was coronated king of Judah. The beginning of his royal career was excellent. He pleased God in many ways after the example of his father Amaziah. He got very after the example of his father Amaziah. He got very far close to God by intimacy and associating with prophets of God. God prospered him.

2Chro. 26:1, 4-5: Then all the people of Judah took Uzziah, who was sixteen years old, and made him king in the room of his father Amaziah" "And he did that which was right in the sight of the LORD, according to all that his father Amaziah did. And he sought God in the days of Zechariah, who had understanding in the visions of God: and as long as he sought the LORD, God made him to prosper.

In his days was Zechariah who had understanding of the visions of God. He got very close to him and God continued to prosper him. Uzziah did many exploits. He was the first king to invent engine to war. He became very famous as strong enemy nations bowed to him.

2Chro. 26:6-8: And he went forth and warred against the Philistines, and brake down the wall of Gath, and the wall of

Jabneh, and the wall of Ashdod, and built cities about Ashdod, and among the Philistines. And God helped him against the Philistines, and against the Arabians that dwelt in Gur-baal, and the Mehunims. And the Ammonites gave gifts to Uzziah: and his name spread abroad even to the entering in of Egypt; for he strengthened himself exceedingly.

Over eighty priests of God withstood Uzziah in the temple. They warned him that trespassing the order of worship was dangerous. Instead of a humble heart and a repentant spirit, Uzziah was very angry with them and continued in his trespass. Obviously, the reaction of Uzziah showed that he was no longer interested in the things of God as the precepts had been laid. God struck him with leprosy, and the end began for a once successful king.

2Chro. 26:16-19: But when he was strong, his heart was lifted up to his destruction: for he transgressed against the LORD his God, and went into the temple of the LORD to burn incense upon the altar of incense. And Azariah the priest went in after him, and with him fourscore priests of the LORD, that were valiant men: And they withstood Uzziah the king, and said unto him, It appertaineth not unto thee, Uzziah, to burn incense unto the LORD, but to the priests the sons of Aaron, that are consecrated to burn incense: go out of the sanctuary; for thou hast trespassed;

neither shall it be for thine honour from the LORD God. Then Uzziah was wroth, and had a censer in his hand to burn incense: and while he was wroth with the priests, the leprosy even rose up in his forehead before the priests in the house of the LORD, from beside the incense altar

Isaiah initially saw visions in the early days of Uzziah.

Isa. 1:1: The vision of Isaiah the son of Amoz, which he saw concerning Judah and Jerusalem in the days of Uzziah, Jotham, Ahaz, and Hezekiah, kings of Judah.

·By the time his ministry got to chapter six, Isaiah made a startling confession. He had lost the vision of God until Uzziah died. There are many commercial prophets and ministers of the gospel today. They are fed by Uzziahs who have lost respect for the things of God. They have lost their visions and revelations. The life of their Uzziahs is the death of their visions. The spirit of Uzziah is therefore the one that blocks divine visions from reaching men. This spirit must be dealt with. It must die.

I shared this testimony somewhere on a Sunday. A family had six boys. Five of them married and their five wives were barren. The sixth boy was a spiritual radical. He prayed that his Uzziah must die because he didn't want to have a similar experience like his brothers. As he prayed, the Lord told him not to go near his wife in the first seven days after his wedding. He was told to just continue in prayer. Although he found the instruction had, he made up his mind to do as God said.

When he came back from honeymoon, he told his wife that they needed to pray. The woman started complaining. He didn't go near her. On the third day, she began to cry that he didn't tell her he had a problem. On the seventh day prayer, there was news that his mother was sick, dying and confessing. The woman said it was their agreement in witchcraft coven for her to take the boy's sperm on the third day after wedding and bank it. The implication of it would be that the brother would be childless. She confessed being responsible for the barrenness of the five others. She said since she couldn't bring the sperm of the sixth boy, her life had to go for it, so she died. Stop a while and take your first decree.

- I decree my Uzziah to die now in the name of Jesus.

THE EVIL VOW

We are moving on to the second decree. Let me explain the background to you. There is what is called the vow of the Egyptians against the children of Israel. Everything about the vow was evil and wicked. The children of Israel just left Egypt, heeding for the promised land. The Egyptians pursued them with a vow to bring them back into bondage again.

Exo. 15:9: *The enemy said, I will pursue, I will overtake, I will divide the spoil; my lust shall be satisfied upon them; I will draw my sword, my hand shall destroy them.*

Their evil determination is found in the expression "I will, I will, I will." Spiritual Egyptians are real. They want to stop you from reaching your Canaan land. They have sworn and vowed to stop you. Therefore, you need to issue a decree to eliminate them. As the Egyptians pursued Israel with a vow, there was a counter – vow of heaven against them.

The Egyptians had not learnt their lessons. They forgot the experience of the ten plagues that came upon them because of the children of Israel. What this reveals is that some enemies can be stubborn. After seeing the hand of God's judgment they may want to advance in their wicked plot. The verdict of heaven against all such enemies is that they should be buried in the red sea. Pray:

* You unrepentant pursuers, die in Jesus' name.

The determination of the enemies is to their own hurt. The Egyptians should have been afraid to see the Red sea part ways. They should have feared to pursue the Israelites into the sea. They were no longer conscious of these wonders as a warning from above. The spirit of madness from the Lord had come upon them to destroy them. Don't worry about the sworn determination of your enemies, God may only be encouraging them to advance to their destruction.

Chapter Five
THE UNCHALLENGEABLE VICTORY

In chapter fifteen verse ten of Exodus, the decree to drown the Egyptian had been issued.

Exo. 15:10: Thou didst blow with thy wind, the sea covered them: they sank as lead in the mighty waters.

The destruction of the Egyptian resulted into the victory dance of the children of Israel. You have to issue a decree against your Egyptians to celebrate your victory. The Egyptians represent demonic powers in all their ramifications and Pharaoh represents a stubborn pursuer

When I was in England, a brother was there for his Ph.D. for eight years, he didn't achieve anything. Imagine somebody who had his first degree, masters degree, yet he could not complete a three year Ph. D programme in eight years. Those days, I used to be spiritually more troublesome than now. When I learnt of his case, I chose to pay him a visit. His 27 years old wife looked like she was in her fifties. The problem was too much for her.

I met her and requested to see her husband who was in the room, crying and starving because of his frustration. The man was reluctant to meet me at first.

He wanted to be sure I wasn't his church member where he said he had enemies as well. I introduced myself as brother Daniel from African Christian Fellowship. When he eventually came out, I encouraged him that we could issue decrees to change the situation. And we started praying. As I kept going there to pray, God revealed to me that the person harassing this man was a neighbour living downstairs. Surprisingly, he too was a Nigerian. For your information, Nigerians carry sacrifices aboard. Herbalists are sponsored abroad for spiritual assistance. Recently, somebody phoned me from abroad that I should be praying seriously for him, because he found a sacrifice in front of his house.

Back to the story of the man I was telling you, I went downstairs to confront the adversary. I loved making serous spiritual troubles in those days. I greeted him and said, "It will be nice if you stop harassing this man upstairs." He immediately warned me that, "You this young boy, leave the devil alone and have your peace." I replied, "Point of correction sir: One, the devil can not rest. Two, he cannot leave anybody alone until death. Only the dead are free from satan's troubles." I continued, "If you leave the devil alone, it means you allow his activities to continue without challenge."

He threatened again, saying "The man has not seen anything yet. I wake up every 12.00 midnight and chant his name." I quickly interrupted him that, "Those charms won't work anymore." Then he ordered me to walk out. I said no problem, but that when next I visited, it would be a time to rejoice and celebrate the victory of the superior power. I left his apartment and continued my prayers with the victim.

Suddenly, God intervened. The white man who had vowed not to see his face anymore called him to defend his thesis, after eight years. We started rejoicing. The man stopped starving and the beauty of his wife began to return. We still continued in prayers. On the previous day to his final examination, I had a revelation. God told me, "slide", which is a specimen to be viewed under a microscope.

I asked the man if he had slides. He said yes. He had over one hundred under his bed because he did zoology. I asked him if any had been lost. He said no. The white man was supposed to ask him questions on his thesis, but for the first time, he informed the external examiner that everything the man was saying was from his memory. He said all Nigerians are liars and that the man didn't have slides. He got to the examination room, dressed in a suit. A white man sat before him with his glasses. Then he said to him, "Hello, how are you? You are putting on a fine suit." He said thank you sir.

The white man went on, "sit down. Give me a cup of tea." The brother did. "Do you want some?", the white man asked? He said no. "The first question," the examiner said, "Can I have a look at your slides?" "How long will it take you to bring them?" he continued. He replied, "About an hour sir." The white man said, "While I continue drinking my tea, go and fetch them?" Quickly, the man examined them one by one. For two hours, he abandoned his cup of tea and concentrated on the slides. At the end of it all, he smiled and said, "Congratulations!" There is no man under heaven who can stand against the heavenly decree. Stop again and issue the second decree.

- I decree that every stubborn pursuer of my life and powers that represent Egypt and Pharaoh, die now in the name of Jesus.

This man was pursued from Nigeria to England. He was pursued right into the examination hall. But a heavenly decree put an end to all activities of the enemy in his life.

There is another spirit you have to deal with in your life by issuing another decree. It is called the spirit of Herod. Look at the activities of the spirit of Herod in the reference below.

Matt. 2:16-18: Then Herod, when he saw that he was mocked of the wise men, was exceeding wroth, and sent forth, and slew all the children that were in Bethlehem, and in all the coasts thereof, from two years old and under, according to the time which he had diligently inquired of the wise men. Then was fulfilled that which was spoken by Jeremy the prophet, saying, In Rama was there a voice heard, lamentation, and weeping, and great mourning, Rachel weeping for her children, and would not be comforted, because they are not.

The spirit of Herod is a killer of good things at infant stage. King Herod killed many children because he wanted to get at Jesus when the Lord was a baby. Another king Herod cut the head of John the Baptist. There was another herod who mocked Jesus. It was yet another Herod who killed James the brother of John in Acts Chapter twelve. This same Herod went beyond his boundary. He arrested Peter and was getting ready to kill him too. But Peter became a seed of corn in a corked bottle standing before a chicken.

Acts 12:19: And when Herod had sought for him, and found him not, he examined the keepers, and commanded that they should be put to death. And he went down from Judea to Caesarea, and there abode.

Peter was miraculously delivered from the prison of Herod. But Herod did not see it as a miracle. He thought the prison keepers aided the escape of the apostle. He ordered them to be killed. In looking for only one Peter, Herod killed sixteen innocent people. One day, king Herod delivered an oratorical speech and men gave him the glory of God. He accepted the glory and heaven struck.

Acts 12:21-23: And upon a set day Herod, arrayed in royal apparel, sat upon his throne, and made an oration unto them. And the people gave a shout, saying, It is the voice of a god, and not of a man. And immediately the angel of the Lord smote him, because he gave not God the glory: and he was eaten of worms, and gave up the ghost.

The spirit of Herod is a destroyer, a killer of prospects, amputators of potentials and haters of the glory to come. Heaven is against the spirit of Herod. You are going to issue a decree for heaven to act upon. You could follow the example in the text above to put

your decree together.

- I decree angelic slap upon my Herod and strange worms to eat him up in the name of Jesus.

THE SPIRIT OF BALAAM

The spirit of Balaam is the fourth spirit you have to issue a decree against. The Bible explains the activities of these spirits in a way they can be understood.

Num. 22:5-6: He sent messengers therefore unto Balaam the son of Beor to Pethor, which is by the river of the land of the children of his people, to call him, saying, Behold, there is a people come out from Egypt: behold, they cover the face of the earth, and they abide over against me: Come now therefore, I pray thee, curse me this people; for they are too mighty for me: peradventure I shall prevail, that we may smite them, and that I may drive them out of the land: for I wot that he whom thou blessest is blessed, and he whom thou cursest is cursed.

The spirit of Balaam represents the hired cursers, evil counselors, and satanic assistants. It was by the counsel of Balaam that the children of Israel went into sin to prepare them for defeat. Eventually, a decree was issued against Balaam and he was slain with the sword. Read the story in numbers chapter thirty one.

There was a brother whom somebody visited in his workshop as if the fellow wanted to buy something. Unknown to him, the visitor had been hired to curse him by another person who felt offended by him. Over a little disagreement, the man said to the brother; "One kobo will not meet another in your hands." The brother though it was a joke, so he said, "You too, one kobo will not meet another in your hands," and forgot to add "in Jesus name." As the man was going, he took some sand in front of the brother's shop, cursed it and went away. The next day, the brother noted that customers would come, peep in and go away including his very regular ones.

Debts began to pile up. He was using his little sales to off-set the growing debts. Then one day, he approached one of his faithful customers and asked, "why do you stop buying from me?" The customer said, I don't know. I don't just feel like buying from you anymore. Even as I am talking with you now. I feel like running away." It became clear to the brother that there was a serious problem. He prayed aggressively ran to his shop and poured anointing oil around it. He returned the curses to sender. Things changed miraculously. The problem he has now is that he does not have enough products to sell to his customers.

The spirit of Balaam is the distributors of verbal poisons. Get ready to issue a decree against them. The brother prayed and the law of substitution took place. He became rich and the one who came to curse him became the beggar.

- I pray thus: You spirit of Balaam working against me should swallow your own poison now in the name of Jesus.

EVIL CONSPIRACY

The fifth spirit you are going to issue a decree against is called the spirit of Korah, Dathan and Abiram. This spirit is behind evil planning and evil conspiracy.

Num. 16:3: And they gathered themselves together against Moses and against Aaron, and said unto them, Ye take too much upon you, seeing all the congregation are holy, every one of them, and the LORD is among them: wherefore then lift ye up yourselves above the congregation of the LORD?.

These men conspired against Moses. They drew an evil plan to contest the claims of Moses in ministry work. They felt Moses was going too much unchallenged. They tried to convince the people that there was nothing happening in the ministry of Moses that was not happening in theirs. They tried to undermine Moses and his ministry. But a decree went forth against them.

Num. 16:32: And the earth opened her mouth, and swallowed them up, and their houses, and all the men that appertained unto Korah, and all their goods

Many years ago, some evil conspirators felt the Church of God was getting too much to contain. They planned to take a corpse to a particular church premises and report the matter to the police to implicate the church. They got a corpse ready and at 5.00 am, they arrived the church. There used to be a morning service at 6.00 a.m. in those days, which is not common nowadays. Either people won't wake up or armed robbers would hinder their freedom of movement.

At the church, the conspirators met a man whose body was fire in a white garment. They were surprised that the garment was not consumed by the fire. The angel told them to keep carrying the corpse till the children of God would gather. Their hands become glued to it. They tried to run or drop the corpse, but it wasn't possible.

The first set of worshippers began to arrive for the usual morning service. They instantly recognized the conspirators as emissaries of a particular king. The worshippers raised an alarm and challenged them to dare drop the corpse. The conspirators said that they couldn't because a man in a white garment had glued their hands to it. A decree was issued against the spirit of Korah, Dathan and Abiram. The police arrested them and the house of God was at peace.

PRAY!
- I decree that every spirit of evil conspiracy against me be swallowed whole by the ground in the name of Jesus.

We are moving on to decree number six now. As the military has various numbers of decrees, so we have our decrees too. We have considered five of them. Let me introduce you to the sixth decree. It is against the spirit of Sanballat and Tobiah who did not want the walls of Jerusalem to be rebuilt. This spirit motivated opposition against Nehemiah in carrying out a divine agenda. The spirits of Sanballat and Tobiah are spirits that hinder people from fulfilling a divine purpose.

Neh. 2:19: But when Sanballat the Horonite, and Tobiah the

servant, the Ammonite, and Geshem the Arabian, heard it, they laughed us to scorn, and despised us, and said, What is this thing that ye do? will ye rebel against the king?.

- **I decree shame upon every spirit of Sanballat and Tobiah working against me in the name of Jesus.**

The last decree in this series is decree number seven. By this decree, you are going to deal with the spirit of Goliath. These are gigantic problems that stand to threaten people. The spirits of Goliath are problems that make you to wonder how they will ever go. The stature of Goliath alone was a problem to the army of Israel.

1Sam. 17:4-7: And there went out a champion out of the camp of the Philistines, named Goliath, of Gath, whose height was six cubits and a span. And he had an helmet of brass upon his head, and he was armed with a coat of mail; and the weight of the coat was five thousand shekels of brass. And he had greaves of brass upon his legs, and a target of brass between his shoulders. And the staff of his spear was like a weaver's beam; and his spear's head weighed six hundred shekels of iron: and one bearing a shield went before him.

The decree you issue will bring down any Goliath. The stature of Goliath is not as important as you decree against him.

- I decrees the stones of fire to enter into the head of my Goliath in the name of Jesus.

When your Goliath is down, your David will take off its head. Let me draw another experience from England. I was preaching to a boy who used to laugh me to scorn. Sometimes, he would say; "Daniel, you brought your religious devotedness from Nigeria to England?" The person was a fist class brain. He made first class in his first degree and a distinction in his masters degree. But an educated sinner will only become more wicked, because his education will teach him latest devices of wickedness. No matter the level or class of education of sinner, his status as a sinner remains the same before God.

One day, I got letter from His majesty's prison. It shocked me because I didn't know anybody there. I read the letter, asking me to buy apple and some other items. Then I got to the subscription of the letter and was greatly surprised to find out who the writer was. It was the friend I'd been preaching the gospel to for a long time.

My visit to the prison that day made me to know how terrible prison life is. I passed through five iron gates to reach this man. So I asked him, how did you arrive here. He was sober. He acknowledged that if he had listened to a quarter of what I'd been telling him, he wouldn't have gotten to prison.

He had been using cheque books stolen from other people to buy things. He used to send a lot of things to Nigeria. The day the long arm of judgment caught up with him was when he went to eat in a Chinease restaurant. Instead of him to pay, he brought the stolen cheque book and issued a leaf. He didn't know there was alert on stolen cheque books. So, when the restaurateur saw the cheque, they called in the police and he found his way to prison. His people expecting him in Nigeria waited in vain.

Before I finished reminding him that he needed to give his life to Christ, he said he had already done so. I interrogated him about what he was said to have done and he confessed that everything was true. I told him to kneel down and let's pray. After he asked for divine forgiveness, I issued a decree on his behalf.

Then the case went on and on until he was finally charged to court. In the court, some of us sat somewhere, praying. Then the magistrate, a white man, looked at him and said, "First class, first degree. Distinction at Masters level, here in Britain? And you did this thing? There is only one explanation. You are mad. Therefore, I order that you should be deported because of you madness." But we knew he wasn't mad. The decision was because of the decree that had been issued.

No matter how long an evil has been in existence, judgment will catch up with it one day. The reward for a life of sin is punishment in this wrld eternal punishment in the world to come. This is an opportunity for you to surrender your life to Jesus. It is dangerous to declare war against satan as a servant in his service. You must first decamp and be on the side of the Lord Jesus. The spirit and the bride are inviting you. This is your chance for a total change of life.

Rev 22:17: And the Spirit and the bride say, Come. And let him that heareth say, Come. And let him that is athirst come. And whosoever will, let him take the water of life freely.

Chapter Six

PRAYER POINTS FOR WINNERS

1. Let every bitter water flow out of my life. I refuse to retain you in the name of Jesus.

2. Let every teeth biting at my goodness be dashed into pieces in the name of Jesus.

3. All witches on evil assignment upon my life, receive abundant failure in the name of Jesus.

4. Lay your hands on your head) I bind every spirit behind evil blood sacrifice in the name of Jesus.

5. I refuse to inherit any evil thing from my parents.

6. Every Uzziah in my life die in the name of Jesus

7. You the spirit of Egypt and Pharaoh, sink in the Red sea in the name of Jesus.

8. Spirit of Herod, receive the worm of fire in the name of Jesus.

9. You the spirit of Balaam, go back to sender in the name of Jesus.

10. Every spirit of Korah, Dathan and Abiram, let the

ground open and swallow you in the name of Jesus.

11. Every spirit of Sanballat and Tobiah receive shame in the name of Jesus.

12. Every spirit of Goliath, die in the name of Jesus.

13. Every power searching for my face in the mirror die with your mirror in the name of Jesus.

14. Every satanic agreement with household wickedness die in the name of Jesus.

15. Every inherited pollution die in the name of Jesus.

16. Oh God of heavens, arise in your power manifest your glory in the name of Jesus.

17. Every enemy of my promotion, die in the name of Jesus.

18. Every witchcraft gathering working against me, scatter in the name of Jesus.

19. Every arrow of darkness fired into my destiny backfire and die in the name of Jesus.

20. I speak confusion into the camp of my Goliath in the name of Jesus.

21. Every habitation of darkness in my family life I speak desolation against you in the name of Jesus.

22. Every local Jericho blocking my breakthroughs die in the name of Jesus.

23. Woe unto every vessel dedicated against my life to demote me, in the name of Jesus.

24. I speak destruction unto the root of my problem now in the name of Jesus.

25. I speak paralysis unto the branch of every problem in my life in the name of Jesus.

26. Thou root of stubborn problems, roast in the name of Jesus.

27. You problems, dry from the root in the name of Jesus.

28. You root of problems I speak death unto you in the name of Jesus.

29. Woe unto every witchcraft programme targeted against my life in the name of Jesus.

30. Every tree planted by familiar spirits in my family, die in the name of Jesus.

31. Every power drinking the blood of my destiny, die in the name of Jesus.

32. Every virtue of my life in any grave yard arise locate me in the name of Jesus.

33. Every witchcraft exchange of my virtue die in the name of Jesus.

34. Every familiar spirit exchange of my destiny die in the name of Jesus.

35. Every marine power exchange of my virtue die in the name of Jesus.

36. Every root of bondage in my life die in the name of Jesus.

Other Publications By Dr. D. K. Olukoya

1. Be Prepared
2. Breakthrough Prayers For Business Professionals
3. Brokenness
4. Born Great, But Tied Down
5. Can God Trust You?
6. Criminals In The House Of God
7. Contending For The Kingdom
8. Dealing With Satanic Exchange
9. Dealing With Local Satanic Technology
10. Dealing With Witchcraft Barbers
11. Dealing With Hidden Curses
12. Dealing With The Evil Powers Of Your Father's House
13. Dealing With Unprofitable Roots
14. Dealing With Tropical Demons
15. Deliverance: God's Medicine Bottle
16. Deliverance From The Limiting Powers
17. Deliverance By Fire
18. Deliverance From Spirit Husband And Spirit Wife
19. Deliverance Of The Conscience
20. Deliverance Of The Head
21. Destiny Clinic
22. Drawers Of Power From The Heavenlies
23. Dominion Prosperity
24. Evil Appetite
25. Facing Both Ways
26. Fasting And Prayer
27. Failure In The School Of Prayer
28. For We Wrestle ...
29. Holy Cry

Other Publications By Dr. D. K. Olukoya

30. Holy Fever
31. How To Obtain Personal Deliverance (Second Edition)
32. How To Pray When Surrounded By The Enemies
33. Idols Of The Heart
34. Is This What They Died For?
35. Limiting God
36. Meat For Champions
37. Medicine For Winners
38. Open Heavens Through Holy Disturbance
39. Overpowering Witchcraft
40. Personal Spiritual Check-Up
41. Power Against Coffin Spirits
42. Power Against Destiny Quenchers
43. Power Against Dream Criminals
44. Power Against Local Wickedness
45. Power Against Marine Spirits
46. Power Against Spiritual Terrorists
47. Power Must Change Hands
48. Pray Your Way To Breakthroughs (Third Edition)
49. Prayer Rain
50. Prayer Strategies For Spinsters And Bachelors
51. Prayers To Move From Minimum To Maximum
52. Prayer Warfare Against 70 Mad Spirits
53. Prayers To Destroy Diseases And Infirmities
54. Praying Against The Spirit Of The Valley
55. Praying To Dismantle Witchcraft
56. Release From Destructive Covenants
57. Revoking Evil Decrees
58. Satanic Diversion Of The Black Race
59. Silencing The Birds Of Darkness

Other Publications By Dr. D. K. Olukoya

60. Smite The Enemy And He Will Flee
61. Spiritual Warfare And The Home
62. Strategic Praying
63. Strategy Of Warfare Praying
64. Students In The School Of Fear
65. The Battle Against The Spirit Of Impossibility
66. The Dinning Table Of Darkness
67. The Enemy Has Done This
68. The Evil Cry Of Your Family Idol
69. The Fire Of Revival
70. The Great Deliverance
71. The Internal Stumbling Block
72. The Lord Is A Man Of War
73. The Mystery Of Mobile Curses
74. The Mystery Of The Mobile Temple
75. The Prayer Eagle
76. The Pursuit Of Success
77. The Seasons Of Life
78. The Star In Your Sky
79. The Secrets Of Greatness
80. The Serpentine Enemies
81. The Skeleton In Your Grandfather's Cupboard
82. The Slow Learners
83. The Snake In The Power House
84. The Spirit Of The Crab
85. The Tongue Trap
86. The Way Of Divine Encounter
87. The Wealth Transfer Agenda
88. The Unconquerable Powers
89. The Vagabond Spirit
90. Tied Down In The Spirits
91. Unprofitable Foundations

Other Publications By Dr. D. K. Olukoya

92. Victory Over Satanic Dreams (Second Edition)
93. Violent Prayers Against Stubborn Situations
94. War At The Edge Of Breakthroughs
95. Wasting The Wasters
96. When God Is Silent
97. Wealth Must Change Hands
98. When You Are Knocked Down
99. Woman! Thou Art Loosed.
100. Your Battle And Your Strategy
101. Your Foundation And Destiny
102. Your Mouth And Your Deliverance
103. Adura Agbayori (Yoruba Version Of The Second Edition Of Pray Your Way To Breakthroughs)
104. Awon Adura Ti Nsi Oke Nidi (Yoruba Prayer Book)
105. Pluie De Prières
106. Esprit Vagabondage
107. En Finir Avec Les Forces Maléfiques De La Maison De Ton Père
108. Que l'envoutement périsse
109. Frappez l'adversaire Et Il Fuira
110. Comment Recevoir La Délivrance Du Mari Et De La Femme De Nuit
112. Comment Se delvrer Soi-même
113. Pouvoir Centre Les Terroristes Spirituels
114. Prières De Percées Pour Les Hommes D'affaires
115. Prier Jusqu'a Remporter La Victoire
116. Prières Violentes Pour Humilier Les Problemes Opiniâtres
117. Le Combat Spirituel Et Le Foyer
118. Bilan Spirituel Personnel

Other Publications By Dr. D. K. Olukoya

119. Victoire Sur Les Rêves Sataniques
120. Prayers That Bring Miracles
121. Let God Answer By Fire
122. Prayers To Mount With Wings As Eagles
123. Prayers That Bring Explosive Increase
124. Prayers For Open Heavens
125. Prayer To Make You Fulfill Your Divine Destiny
126. Prayers That Make God To Answer And Fight By Fire
127. Prayers That Bring Unchallengeable Victor˙ And Breakthrough Rainfall Bombardments

ALL OBTAINABLE AT:

1. 11, Gbeto Street, Off Iyana Church Bus Stop, Iwaya Road, Iwaya, Yaba,. P. O. Box. 12272, Ikaja, Lagos.
2. MFM International Bookshop, 13 Olasimbo, Street, Onike, Yaba, Lagos.
3. IPFY Music Connections Limited, 48, Opebi, Salvation Bus Stop (234-1-4719471, 234-0833056093)
4. All Mfm Church Branches Nationwide And Christian Bookstores.

www.ingramcontent.com/pod-product-compliance
Lightning Source LLC
Chambersburg PA
CBHW060852050426
42453CB00008B/944

Medicine For Winners

If there is any area of life where spiritual warfare is needed, it is in the area of achieving success and winning in life. This book offers uncommon nuggets which if utilized will lead the reader to the realm of outstanding success. Medicine For Winners will surely enable you to cultivate the habit of succeeding. The spiritual factors necessary for dealing with powers behind failure are clearly outlined. The book also contains powerful prayer points, which will make the reader a winner in all areas of life. It is a must read for those who want to manifest the winning lifestyle.

About the Author

Dr. D. K. Olukoya is the General Overseer of the Mountain of Fire and Miracles Ministries and The Battle Cry Christian Ministries.

The Mountain of Fire and Miracles Ministries' Headquarters is the largest single Christian congregation in Africa with attendance of over 120,000 in single meetings.

MFM is a full gospel ministry devoted to the revival of Apostolic signs, Holy Ghost Fireworks, miracles and the unlimited demonstration of the power of God to deliver to the uttermost. Absolute holiness within and without as spiritual insecticide and pre-requisite for heaven is openly taught. MFM is a do-it-yourself Gospel Ministry, where your hands are trained to wage war and your fingers to do battle.

Dr. Olukoya holds a first class honours degree in Micro-biology from the University of Lagos and a PhD in Molecular Genetics from the University of Reading, United Kingdom. As a researcher, he has over seventy scientific publications to his credit.

Anointed by God, Dr. Olukoya is a prophet, evangelist, teacher and preacher of the Word. His life and that of his wife, Shade and their son Elijah Toluwani are living proofs that all power belongs to God.